IMAGES OF
LANCASHIRE &
CHESHIRE RAILWAYS

IMAGES OF
LANCASHIRE &
CHESHIRE RAILWAYS

CLASSIC PHOTOGRAPHS FROM
THE MAURICE DART RAILWAY COLLECTION

HALSGROVE

First published in Great Britain in 2010

British Library Cataloguing-in-Publication Data
A CIP record for this title is available from the British Library

ISBN 978 0 85704 056 5

HALSGROVE
Halsgrove House,
Ryelands Industrial Estate,
Bagley Road, Wellington, Somerset TA21 9PZ
Tel: 01823 653777   Fax: 01823 216796
email: sales@halsgrove.com

Part of the Halsgrove group of companies
Information on all Halsgrove titles is available at: www.halsgrove.com

Printed and bound in Great Britain by SRP Ltd., Exeter

CONTENTS

Introduction 6

Acknowledgements and Reference Sources 8

1. Beyer Garratts and the Ljungstrom loco 9

2. 2–10–0 and 0–8–4 Tank 11

3. 2–8–0s 12

4. 0–8–0s 19

5. Pacific 4–6–2s 27

6. 4–6–0s 34

7. 2–6–4 Tanks 43

8. LNER 2–6–2s 45

9. 2–6–2 Tanks 46

10. 2–6–0s 48

11. 0–6–2 Tanks 52

12. LMS, Midland and L & Y 0–6–0s 55

13. LNER 0–6–0s 62

14. GWR 0–6–0 Tanks 67

15. LMS and LNWR 0–6–0 Tanks 71

16. L & Y 0–6–0 Tanks 73

17. LNER 0–6–0 Tanks 79

18. LNER 4–4–2 Tanks 81

19. GWR 4–4 –0s 83

20. LMS 4–4–0s 85

21. LNER 4–4–0s 90

22. 2–2–2–2 and 2–4–2 Tanks 95

23. LMS 0–4–4 Tanks 105

24. 2–4–0s, 2–2–2–0 and 2–4–0 Tank 109

25. 0–4–2 Tank and LMS 0–4–0 Tanks 113

26. Service and Preserved Locos, Shed Scenes and Accident 121

27. LMS Electric Sets 129

28. Electric Locos 131

29. Diesel Locos 138

30. Liverpool Overhead Railway and Industrial Locos 143

Location Index 160

INTRODUCTION

At a very early age I was taken to Dockyard Halt, near Devonport and soon afterwards to St Budeaux GWR station to 'watch trains'. I was taught to remember the names of three engines that passed through. At home there was a Hornby Gauge '0' model railway. Most Saturday afternoons my parents would take me with them from St Budeaux to either Devonport, reached by tram, or Plymouth, to which we caught a 'motor train' to Millbay. So my interest in railways steadily developed. During the summers of 1937, 1938 and 1939, the three of us spent a week travelling by train to Torquay, Paignton or Goodrington, with sometimes a venture to Kingswear and across to Dartmouth on the 'MEW', or to Dawlish Warren. We used a family holiday runabout ticket for the week and set out from St Budeaux on an excursion train that ran daily from Saltash to Paignton and which, from memory, was usually hauled by a Castle class locomotive to Newton Abbot. From our front windows at Higher St Budeaux I was able to watch trains in the distance as they climbed towards the Devon side of the Royal Albert Bridge. They could also be seen as they rounded the curves west of Saltash station. I asked my father on one occasion why we did not go to Cornwall instead of to Paignton and he replied that it was better to go up the line. This was probably because there was a daily excursion train from Saltash to Paignton although we frequently had to change trains at Newton Abbot and cross over the footbridge. My father would bring home books about railways. They had been loaned to him for me to look at and they contained many photographs of railway subjects. During the Second World War, following the second batch of blitz raids on Plymouth when many schools were damaged, I was evacuated to Bude by train from Friary. I stood in the corridor for most of the way to "see where I was going" much to the consternation of the WVS ladies who were accompanying us. I recall seeing a tank engine, at what I later learned was Meldon Quarry, carrying 500S on its tank side. This was the T class 'Service loco'. Whilst at Bude I began to hear about places such as Holsworthy and Okehampton, which I had passed through on the train. Evacuation to Bude was followed by a short period back at St Budeaux after which I spent two years at St Austell, using trains to and from North Road. Whilst there, at the evacuated Grammar school, I met many older boys who were railway enthusiasts and my 'railway education' commenced properly.

My father had been transferred from Devonport to the Dockyard at Gibraltar during 1943, and in the summer of 1947 I went there by sea for a holiday for several weeks. My father was an amateur photographer and he taught me to use a box camera. I immediately started taking photographs of Gibraltar Dockyard locomotives from a balcony! On returning to St Budeaux I found my father's two old cameras and managed to obtain a film for each. A large folding Kodak that used A-122 film turned out to have a pin hole in the bellows, only discovered when the results of the first film were seen. This made it unusable. The other was an old Box Brownie which had a push-over lever shutter release and had one good and one faulty viewfinder that showed two images, one above the other. I persevered with this but did not know enough to achieve much success. I tried to record trains passing through St Budeaux and went to Laira shed late in September and took photos, some against the low evening sun. Still, we all had to learn by experience. With those which I had taken at Gibraltar, this was the start of my collection of railway photographs. I saved my pocket money and managed to go on a few Saturday trips to Exeter and as a holiday treat I was allowed to make trips to Bristol and Salisbury. In January 1948 my mother and I joined my father in Gibraltar which involved sailing from and to Liverpool. This was my introduction to Cheshire's and Lancashire's railways even though we were in darkness after departing from Crewe on the outward journey. After checking into a nearby hotel I ventured down to Lime Street station in snow for a short time but did not explore much in the darkness. A few years later we returned from Lime Street to Plymouth North Road in daylight and I saw more of the railways in the two counties. In 1952 I spent time in both counties visiting locomotive sheds. Later, my employment took me to lodge at St Austell where I finally took up permanent residence. As time progressed I was able to buy better cameras and commenced longer railway trips to places further afield. During 1953 friends moved back from Plymouth to Westhoughton and I spent several holidays based there and widened my knowledge of the Lancashire's railways considerably. I was fascinated by the many old L & Y locomotive types operating around Bolton. Over a period of years due to changes in county boundaries some locations which were originally in Lancashire have moved to Cheshire but as both counties are included in this book this is irrelevant. My railway interest widened from purely collecting engine names and numbers to encompass signalling and railway history. This was progressed by meeting more very knowledgeable older railway enthusiasts and railwaymen, many of whom became lifelong friends of mine. I developed a desire to obtain photographs of some of the locomotives that I had seen in my early years, so the process of searching for and purchasing photos commenced. As my interest and knowledge grew, so likewise did the quest for more photos. This now encompassed all of Devon and Cornwall and large sections of Wales, along with various classes of locomotives from all over the country. An interest in narrow gauge and industrial railways developed. So the 'Archive' steadily grew from filling an expanding suitcase to occupying a considerable expanse of shelf space in two rooms. When it was suggested that I compile some books making use of some of these images I thought that it would be a great idea as many of them, to the best of my knowledge, had not previously been used in publications. Previous books covered Devon, Cornwall, Somerset and Dorset, Wiltshire and Hampshire. With so many photos available the choice has been difficult but constraints such as copyright and previous use have been considered. This is not an attempt to include every location or type of locomotive that has worked in the area but is simply a selection from my collection. As the collection has been collected by me personally my own particular interests and likings for certain locomotive types are reflected by some sections containing larger selections of photos than others. Some older historic images are included but I have attempted to give a good overall coverage of the area from around 1900 to the present day. I have included a selection of electrics and diesels and some industrial locomotives to attempt to cater for all interests. So many photographs of the preservation era have been published that I have mainly avoided this period. I have also used some items which are not photographically perfect but merit inclusion because of their content. These images may be of great interest to modellers of historic locomotives with period layouts. As this book features images from my personal collection, the layout follows the order in which the collection is arranged. This follows locomotive wheel arrangement and types from the largest downwards in decreasing order of size, with a few exceptions. It is a system that was used in the past by several notable authors that presents a markedly different layout to the now standard practice of following routes geographically. Readers seeking photos at specific locations should refer to the index of locations at the end of the book. I have attempted to make the captions detailed without delving too deeply into railway history or becoming too technical. Any errors that are discovered are purely attributable to myself. I trust that within the contents there is material to cater for most railway interests and that memories of a bygone age of railways will be recalled.

ACKNOWLEDGEMENTS

I express special thanks to my friend Kenneth Brown for permission to reproduce photos taken by him. Likewise I express thanks for permission to use photos which I have purchased from the collections of the Stephenson Locomotive Society, The Locomotive Club of Great Britain (Ken Nunn collection) and Rail Archive Stephenson (Photomatic). Also my thanks and apologies are proffered to other photographers whose work has been used and not credited. Where no credit is given the photographer is unknown. I also extend my thanks to Steve Jenkins for advice when describing some of the carriage and wagon stock. I am also indebted to Simon Butler of Halsgrove for suggesting the idea of this series of books.

REFERENCE SOURCES

A Detailed History of British Railways Standard Steam Locomotives. RCTS.

A Regional History of the Railways of Great Britain. Vol.10. The North West.
        Geoffrey Holt. David & Charles.

British Railways Locomotive Stock Changes and Withdrawal Dates. 1948 –1968.
        Michael McManus.

British Railways Steam Locomotives 1948–1968. Hugh Longworth. OPC.

An Illustrated History of LMSR Locomotives. Essary & Jenkinson. OPC and SLP.

Locomotives of the LNER. RCTS.

LMSR, LNER and BR Locomotive Allocations for Various Years. RCTS.

The Allocation History of BR Diesels & Electrics. Roger Harris.

The Directory of Railway Stations. R.V.J. Butt.

GWR Locomotive Allocations. First and Last Sheds. 1922–1967. J.W.P. Rowledge.

British Locomotive Names of the Twentieth Century. H.C. Casserley.

My personal notebooks dating from 1945.

1

BEYER GARRATTS AND THE LJUNGSTROM LOCO

The LMS Garratts visited Crewe Works and the sole LNER Garratt did likewise at Gorton. The Ljungstrom loco was an experimental turbo-condensing design built by Beyer Peacock at their Gorton Works.

We commence with a shot taken in August 1938 of LMS 2–6–0 + 0–6–2 Beyer Garratt 7973 in the large yard at Crewe Works awaiting attention. The rotary coal bunker is prominent.

LMS Garratt 47988 which was withdrawn from Hasland shed is in the cutting-up area at Crewe Works on 5 September 1956. Maurice Dart/Transport Treasury.

This is the monster LNER U1 class 2–8–2 + 2–8–2 Garratt 69999 in the yard at Gorton Works on 1 February 1953 when it was shedded at Mexborough. This loco was designed to bank heavy freight trains from Wath yard up Worsborough incline which it did for many years until steam power was replaced by electric locos. It then had a couple of spells banking freight trains up the Lickey incline but spent periods at Gorton Works. Luckily I saw it there on 28 August 1952. It was too far away for me to take a shot of it and it was impossible to gain access to Gorton shed or works without a permit. B.K.B.Green/Initial Photographics.

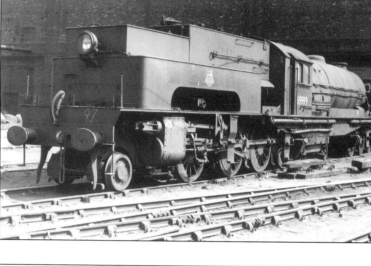

Here is a shot of the other side of 69999 at Gorton Works on 16 August 1953.

This is the strange looking Ljungstrom turbo-condensing loco brand new in the works yard of Beyer Peacock at Gorton in 1926. The wheel arrangement has been described as 4–(2–2)–2 + 0–6–4. Boiler pressure was 285 lb/sq.in. and the driving wheels were of 5ft 3in diameter. The loco reached 70mph. The devices on the front of the smokebox door include two fans. This loco was used on the LMS system for a period. Railway Photographs.

2

2–10–0 AND 0–8–4 TANK

2–10–0s operated in both counties and 0–8–4Ts worked in Lancashire.

Heavy freight 2–10–0 92045 from Bidston shed heads an eastbound train of John Summers bogie hopper wagons through the closed Burton Point station on 26 August 1959. Maurice Dart.

7F 0–8–4T 47937 is near the coal stage at Edge Hill shed where it was based on 18 April 1950. The loco was withdrawn from service on 2 December that year. Lines pass through bridges behind the loco to access the shed buildings.

3
2–8–0s

Representatives of these classes were to be seen in most parts of both counties.

Following the closure of the GWR shed at Chester at the start of February 1958 the locos were serviced at ex LMS sheds in the area. GWR 2800 class 2875 from Westbury shed was a long way from home when recorded at Mold Junction shed on an unknown date in 1961. LMS Black Five 4–6–0s present are, on the left 45386 from Holyhead shed and 44842 which is at home and is mostly hidden behind 2875.

This is a line of engines in the yard at Chester GWR shed on 14 September 1956. On the right is 8750 class 0–6–0PT 9728. the others are, from the right, 2884 class 2–8–0 3820, 8750 class 0–6–0PT 9794, Modified Hall 7921 'EDSTONE HALL' and Manor class 7807 'COMPTON MANOR'. All of these locos were based at Chester. Maurice Dart/Transport Treasury.

Next we look at some of the well known LMS 8F 2–8–0s and start with a loco returned after loan to the War Department. Still carrying its WD number 78588 this loco is at an unknown location near Crewe on 8 October 1949. It was taken over by the WD in August 1942 and worked in Iran where it became Iran State Railway 41–187 and later on was stored at Azzib. It was returned to England and reached Crewe in 1948. Later in 1949 following overhaul it became BR 48039 and was allocated to Rugby.

Locally based 48045 brings a train eastwards through Northwich on 16 September 1955. Maurice Dart/Transport Treasury.

All four of the railway companies built 8Fs during the war. This is Birkenhead's Swindon built 48479 outside Northwich shed on 16 September 1955. Maurice Dart/Transport Treasury.

A friend of mine in Liverpool just happened to live next door to a Locomotive Inspector to whom I was introduced. This acquaintance proved invaluable and during my visits 'several doors' were opened for me so to speak. One of these was to visit Speke Junction shed on 10 February 1968. Before I left Plymouth a few days previously I had heard the weather forecast so took wellington boots with me. So on that day Buxton's 8F 48723 was taking water in snowy conditions. The shedman is attending to the lit brazier by the water column. On the left is Black Five 4–6–0 45280 which had been withdrawn from Birkenhead shed. Maurice Dart/Transport Treasury.

Now we look at a few LNER 2-8-0s and start with O4/3 class 63649 from Gorton shed running westwards as it appoached the closed Burton Point station on 25 August 1960. Maurice Dart/Transport Treasury.

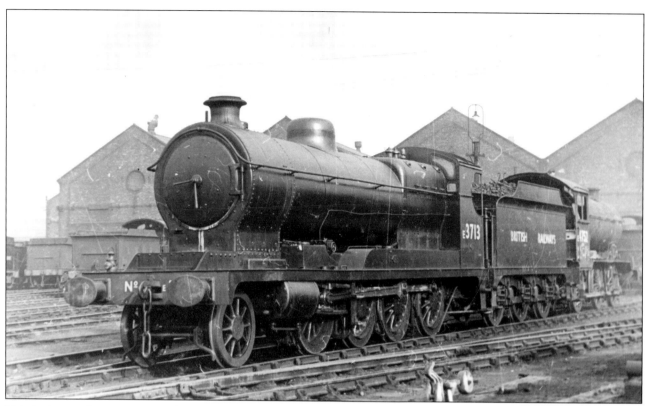

This is the yard at Gorton Works on 12 March 1948. Centrepiece ex-Works is O4/3 class E3713 based at Gorton. To its right, devoid of its tender and awaiting entry to the Works is Ipswich shed's J39/1class 0–6–0 E4752. The E prefix was a temporary measure which preceded the BR re-numbering scheme.

A pair of locos at Bidston shed on 26 August 1952 are local J94 0–6–0ST 68063 and O4/1 class 63722 from Gorton shed. Maurice Dart/Transport Treasury.

An eastbound freight is near Guide Bridge in the 1950s headed by recently ex-Works O4/3 class 63822 from Darnall shed. It is passing a rather ornate signal gantry.

This is a mystery photo which although of somewhat inferior quality is included because of its interesting content. During the First World War many Robinson LNER type 2–8–0s were built for the Railway Operating Division. After hostilities ceased they were returned to this country. Two batches worked on the GWR. However this unidentified loco is passing the yards west of Crewe so may have come across from Shrewsbury. It has fluted buffers and still carries the Westinghouse Pump. It could possibly be working a LNWR Postal train. R.S.Carpenter.

We end this section with a couple of WD 2–8–0s and see 90387 from Rose Grove at Bolton shed on 8 September 1955. Maurice Dart/Transport Treasury.

The WDs were usually notoriously dirty but here is a relatively clean example. Aintree shed on 9 September 1955 was host to Wigan Central shed's 90599 which had just been turned. Maurice Dart/Transport Treasury.

4

0–8–0s

Ex LNWR types worked in both counties. L & Y types and LMS built 'Austin Sevens' were mainly to be found working in Lancashire. LNER types visited Gorton Works.

We commence this section with a look at ex LNWR types. G1 class 0–8–0 49023 rests at home at Springs Branch shed on 9 September 1956. Maurice Dart/Transport Treasury.

Another local G1 class 49378 brings a freight north past Springs Branch Junction on 9 September 1956. Maurice Dart/Transport Treasury.

On 12 September 1955 G2A class 49385 from Springs Branch shed has propelled a brake van up Chequerbent incline and is slowly passing through the closed station. Maurice Dart/Transport Treasury.

After passing through Chequerbent station on 12 September 1955 G2A class 49385 uncoupled from the brake van and set back into the yard to pick up some wagons presenting an opportunity for this rather atmospheric shot. Maurice Dart/Transport Treasury.

On 29 September 1953 Speke Junction's G2 class 49406 is in the yard at Springs Branch shed. The engine is fitted with a Tender cab. Partly hidden by the 0–8–0 is Jubilee class 4–6–0 45604 'CEYLON' from Crewe North. Maurice Dart.

On 12 September 1955 the same loco 49406, which was still allocated to Speke Junction, passes Westhoughton Goods with a westbound freight. Just to the right of the nearest building is an outside framed MR 10T van. Maurice Dart/Transport Treasury.

Now we see a solitary example of an ex L & Y loco. In the 1930s 6F class 30 12729 is inside its home shed at Wigan Central. The loco which is fitted with a Belpaire firebox was withdrawn during 1946.

We next see several of the Fowler 7F locos built by the LMS which were called 'Austin Sevens'. Two of the class, both from Lees shed, Oldham, are outside the east end of Newton Heath shed on 7 September 1956 which was plagued by heavy rain. 49509 is receiving attention with its buffer beam removed. On its right is 49668. Maurice Dart/Transport Treasury.

Also on 7 September 1956 two local engines are outside the east end of Newton Heath shed. On the right is 49624 while head on 49511 has had its front coupled wheels removed. In the left distance is MR 2F 0–6–0 58128 which was also allocated there. Maurice Dart.

At home outside Bolton shed on 8 September 1955 is 49532. Maurice Dart/Transport Treasury.

By late afternoon on 7 September 1956 when I reached Lees shed the rain had stopped. Two locally based engines outside are 49536 and L & Y 3F 0–6–0 52410. Maurice Dart/Transport Treasury.

Locally based 49544 is outside Bolton shed on 1 April 1956. Maurice Dart/Transport Treasury.

Two local engines 49624 and 49511 are outside the east end of Newton Heath shed on 7 September 1956. Bunker first on the left is Stanier 4P 2–6–4T 42557 from Wigan Central shed. Maurice Dart/Transport Treasury.

Later on 7 September 1956 49668 returned home to Lees shed from Newton Heath. Maurice Dart/Transport Treasury.

We end with the solitary LNER example of the type. On 12 March 1948 Q4 class E3243 from Ardsley shed awaits attention outside Gorton Works. One of the Works' Managers watches the photographer who is also viewed from a distance by another member of staff.

5

PACIFIC 4–6–2s

L MS and BR Standard locos worked through both counties on the LMS routes. Visitors appeared during the 1948 Locomotive Exchanges.

The first shot is this section shows a complete stranger to the area. During 1948 a series of Locomotive Exchanges were carried out between the various regions of the newly-formed British Railways to assess the performance of various locomotives. SR West Country class lightweight Pacific 34004 'YEOVIL' from Exmouth Junction shed travelled to Scotland to carry out trials between Perth and Inverness. For the trials it was paired with an LMS tender fitted with a water scoop. As there were no water troughs on the SR system none of their tenders were so fitted. Following the completion of the trials the loco returned south. It was recorded at Crewe North on 17 July 1948 still paired with the LMS tender on its way home.

Next we see some representatives of the LMS 'PRINCESS ROYAL' class locos. 46200 'PRINCESS ROYAL' by now shedded at Carlisle Kingmoor, brings a train formed of BR Mark 1 coaches around the curve as it enters Preston with a train from Scotland in 1962.

I was extremely lucky to be able to take this photo. 46202 'PRINCESS ANNE' from Camden shed waits to start away from Crewe at 3.20pm with the Red Rose express from Euston to Liverpool Lime Street on 29 August 1952. This loco had been rebuilt from the un-named LMS Turbo-motive 6202 and was only two days out from Crewe Works. This was the second day it worked this train whilst 'running in'. When it entered Crewe I was on the famous footbridge which spanned the north end of the station. To obtain this shot I ran across the bridge and down almost to the bottom of the ramp which led to Crewe North shed. This was during my first long distance railway holiday when I stayed away for nine days and borrowed my father's Zeiss-Ikon camera to use instead of my box camera. This loco only worked from 27 August until 8 October as on the later date it was involved in the triple smash at Harrow & Wealdstone. It was the train engine on an express from Manchester London Road which collided with the wreckage of an express from Perth which had run into a local train from Tring. It occurred at 8.20am and this loco was damaged beyond repair. Maurice Dart.

A train entering Crewe from the south during July 1955 is hauled by Edge Hill shed's 46204 'PRINCESS LOUISE'.

We progress now to the Princess Coronation class locos which numbered 38 locos, 29 of which were built with streamlined casings. The streamlining was removed during the early to mid-1940s. An express near Burton & Holme in the late 1930s is headed by streamlined 6223 'PRINCES ALICE'.

On 9 July 1939 streamlined 6228 'DUCHESS OF RUT-LAND' is outside Edge Hill shed.

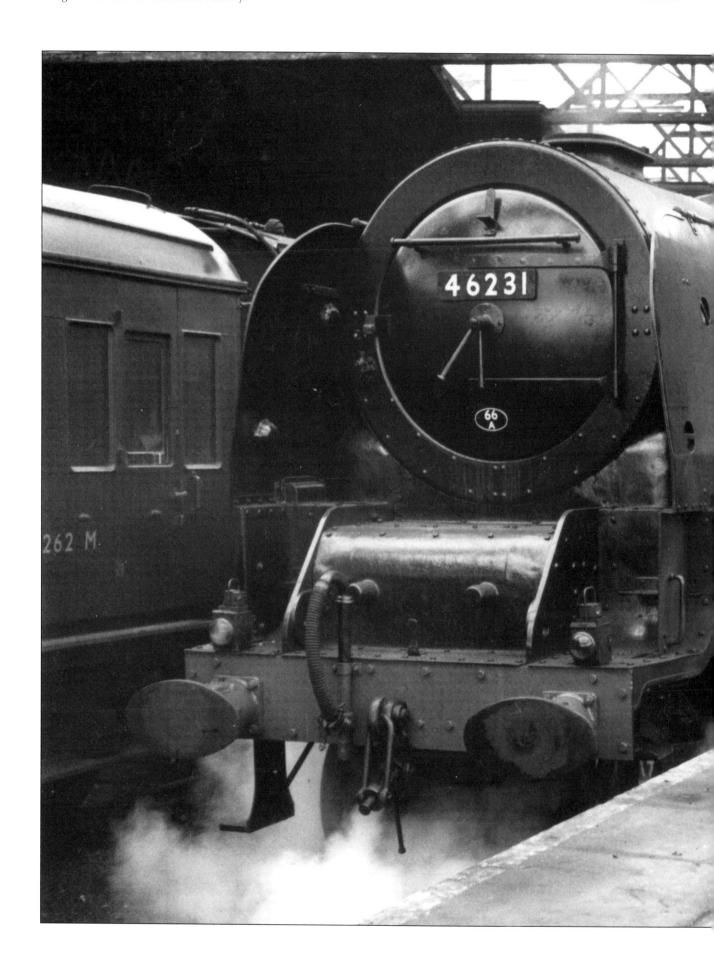

At approximately 6am on 1 June 1958 a long heavy northbound Newspaper train waits to depart from Crewe headed by 46231 'DUCHESS OF ATHOLL' from Polmadie shed. David Pick.

At its home shed, Crewe North on 5 October 1952 is 46233 'DUCHESS OF SUTHERLAND'.

Early in 1961 46245 'CITY OF LONDON' from Camden shed is in the extensive yards at Crewe Works. The engine has obviously recently emerged after receiving an overhaul. In the right distance are withdrawn Fowler 2–6–2Ts 40066 and 40053 which last worked from Willesden and Bedford sheds respectively. British Railways, London Midland Region.

Centrepiece on 1 April 1963 at Crewe Works is 46253 'CITY OF ST ALBANS' which had recently been withdrawn from Crewe North shed. To the right is the front of Stanier 4MT 2–6–4T 42469 from Heaton Mersey shed. R.J.Buckley.

We end this section with Polmadie shed's BR Standard Clan class 72003 'CLAN FRASER' heading an express south past Hest Bank on 21 July 1954.

6

4–6–0s

Examples of locos of this type were widespread throughout both counties.

GWR locos worked to Crewe from both Wellington and Shrewsbury and the GWR possessed a small engine shed at Gresty Lane to service them. Engines which required turning used either of the LMS sheds. On 18 November 1950 5981 'FRENSHAM HALL' from Shrewsbury shed is behind an Ivatt 2–6–2T at Crewe North shed. The GWR S^L°P SHED stencil with raised A and O is prominent. We saw a few rare visiting engines with this code at Laira shed, Plymouth, in the late 1940s. They were mainly 2–8–0s.

GWR locos also reached Manchester over the route from Chester via Frodsham and Warrington Bank Quay. In the mid-1940s the driver of 6816 'FRANKTON GRANGE' which is carrying a BAN (Banbury) shed stencil rests against a buffer in front of his engine as it waits to depart from Manchester Exchange for Chester. I guess that a Grange would have been quite a rare visitor on that route. Some of the platforms of the adjoining Manchester Victoria Station are centre left.

Stafford Road shed's Star class 4053 'PRINCESS ALEXANDRA' takes a southbound train out of Chester General past the GWR loco shed in the early 1950s.

Now comes a selection of LMS locos starting with the Royal Scot class. This loco from Camden shed is carrying the identity 46100 'ROYAL SCOT' at Crewe Works on 19 August 1951. However all is not what it appears to be. 'ROYAL SCOT' was due to visit the USA in 1933 but the loco was in Crewe Works as departure time approached. The problem was overcome by the engine swapping name and number with 6152 'THE KING'S DRAGOON GUARDSMAN'. On return from the USA the change became permanent.

In the late 1950s Longsight shed's 46111 'ROYAL FUSILIER' is on the Manchester lines north of Crewe station, waiting to back in on to a train.

In the 1930s 6119 'LAN-CASHIRE FUSILIER' stands on the Chester lines north of Crewe station adjacent to the Works. On the tender is LMS in the short-lived 'sans serif' livery that was introduced in 1936.

In August 1939 6159 'THE ROYAL AIR FORCE' stands near the turntable at Crewe North shed.

In 1930 an experimental high-pressure loco was constructed using the frames and other features of the Royal Scot class. It was numbered 6399 and was named 'FURY'. During its first trial run a high-pressure steam tube in the cab exploded and the fireman was killed. The loco was taken into Works for modifications and several years later ran some further trials which proved unsatisfactory. In 1936 the loco was rebuilt and emerged as the first of the rebuilt Royal Scots. The loco is inside Crewe Works as originally built carrying an indicator shelter used during its trials.

Here is the engine at the south end of Crewe station in the late 1930s following rebuilding. It has been re-numbered to 6170, re-named 'BRITISH LEGION' and was allocated to Crewe North shed.

Next we see one photo of a member of the Jubilee class. On 3 June 1939 5554 'ONTARIO' which appears to be carrying a 4A (Shrewsbury) shedplate heads a down express near Kirkham & Wesham. R. J. Buckley.

This is 44868 which is one of large class of Black Five locos. The nickname aptly describes the appearance of this loco which was heading west through Bolton Trinity Street on dull wet 10 September 1956. The loco was shedded at Holyhead. Maurice Dart.

Now we come to some photos of the Patriot class. The first two members were rebuilt Claughton class locos. The following forty locos were nominally described as such but incorporated little of the original locos. The last ten were new engines. On 26 April 1949 45508 is approaching Preston from the north. This engine which was allocated to Preston shed never carried a name and was originally numbered 6010.

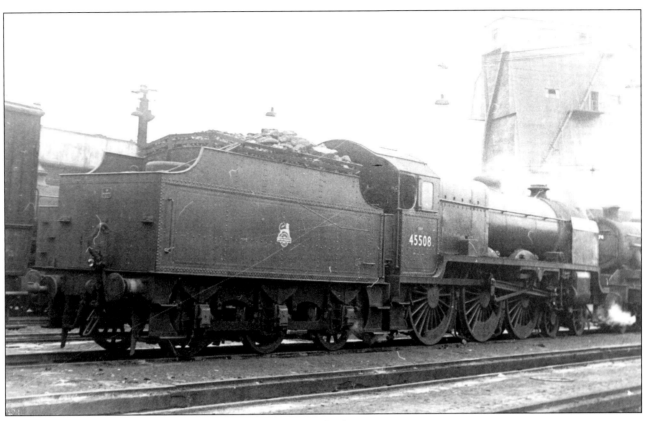

On 12 September 1950 Preston's 45508 is at Patricroft shed.

On 26 April 1949 45519 'LADY GODIVA' heads an express north out of Preston. Originally numbered 6008 it was shedded at Preston.

On 12 September 1950 a southbound express enters Crewe double headed by two Patriots. The pilot is 45537 (ex 6015) 'PRIVATE E. SYKES VC' from Preston shed. The train engine is un-named 5510 (ex 6012) from Crewe North shed.

During a wintry February 1957 Carlisle Kingmoor shed's 45543 'HOME GUARD' stands in snow outside Crewe Works. A. R. Butcher/Top Link Photos.

On 26 November 1954 45546 'FLEETWOOD' is dumped at Crewe North shed. The engine which was allocated to Willesden suffered damage in a smash at Betley Road. R. J. Buckley.

We progress to a few of the older LMS 4–6–0 types starting with Claughton class 5921 'SIR ARTHUR LAWLEY' at Crewe North shed on 14 April 1934. This engine was withdrawn before the year ended. C. L. Hodgetts.

Un-named Prince Of Wales class 25749 from Patricroft shed waits on a train at the west end of Chester station in August 1935. This engine was withdrawn during 1946. An LMS horsebox is in the right background.

On 5 January 1935 Llandudno Junction's Prince Of Wales class 25845 is at Crewe North shed. This was one of five members of the class that were constructed with a raised running plate and outside Walschaerts valve gear. They were nicknamed 'Tishies' because the way the rods moved was reminiscent of movement of a racehorse called 'Tishy' whose legs appeared to be crossed as he ran. This engine was withdrawn during 1947.

We end this section with two LNER 4–6–0s. B2 class 5426 'CITY OF CHESTER' is at Gorton Works following withdrawal during December 1944.

The crew pose in the cab of B7 class 5482 (which became 1395 in November 1946) in 1937 as it waits to go off Gorton shed to work a train to Sheffield. This loco was withdrawn in November 1948.

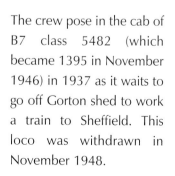

7

2–6–4 TANKS

LMS types worked on that companies lines in both counties. They also operated on the CLC routes.

Fowler 4MT 2359 from Barrow shed waits to depart from Carnforth with a local northbound passenger service on 12 June 1947.

Patricroft shed's Stanier 4MT 42439 has uncoupled from a train at Manchester Exchange on 22 August 1960 and is slowly moving out of the station. Maurice Dart/Transport Treasury.

Stanier 4MT 42447 from Crewe North is at the coal stage at Alsager shed on 30 August 1952. Maurice Dart.

Another Stanier 4MT, 2649 heads a down express at Kirkham & Wesham on 3 June 1939. The engine appears to be carrying a 24E (Blackpool Central) shed plate R. J. Buckley.

8
LNER 2–6–2s

These worked trains over the Woodhead route to Manchester.

Gorton shed's V2 4887 heads an eastbound express at Guide Bridge in the mid 1940s. In November 1946 this engine was re-numbered 916.

This is another shot of Gorton's V2 4887 as it departed from Guide Bridge on the same day.

9

2–6–2 TANKS

GWR locos were to be seen at Chester and Crewe. LMS designed locos and BR Standard types operated in both counties but I have no photos of the latter in my collection.

The crew pose in the cab of GWR 4500 class 4517 for the photographer at Chester GWR shed. As this loco has a small bunker, numberplate on the side tank and no front support struts the photo was most likely taken soon after the engine was sent brand new to Chester shed in February 1908. Real Photographs.

GWR Large Prairie tanks worked to Crewe from Wellington. Here is 5101 class 4158 from Wellington shed at the south end of Crewe station on 5 September 1956. On the left part of Alsager shed's 4F 0–6–0 44503 is visible. Maurice Dart/Transport Treasury.

Engines which had been overhauled at Horwich Works were sent to Bolton shed for 'running in' On 8 September 1955 Stanier 3MT 40155 from Manningham shed rests alongside Bolton shed. Maurice Dart/Transport Treasury.

At Plodder Lane shed, Bolton on 24 April 1949 two of its resident Ivatt 2MT tanks, 41213 and 41215 are outside during a visit by enthusiasts. B. K. B. Green/Initial Photographics.

On 16 September 1955 outside Chester Northgate shed are local Ivatt 2MT 41215 and LNER C13 class 4–4–2T 67430 from Wrexham Rhosddu shed. Maurice Dart.

10

2–6–0s

Locos of GWR, LMS and BR origin worked in both counties. LNER locos worked in Lancashire but I do not possess any photos of them in the county.

GWR 4300 class 6389 runs south through Warrington Bank Quay High Level station in the 1930s on its way back to Chester. A GWR Toad brake van is stabled in the short siding behind the engine.

In the 1930s GWR Aberdare class 2623 heads a long Goods bound for Manchester north through Warrington Bank Quay High Level. This loco was allocated to Chester shed in 1934.

Now we progress to various types of LMS 2–6–0s and see Rose Grove shed's 'Crab' 42716 on Bolton shed on 8 September 1955. Maurice Dart.

Bolton shed's 'Crab' 42723 is on Crewe South shed on 21 April 1963. R. J. Buckley.

Ex Horwich Works 'Crab' 42783 from Nuneaton shed is on an eastbound Goods at Bolton Trinity Street working a 'running in' turn on 30 March 1959. The large goods shed forms a backdrop. Maurice Dart/ Transport Treasury.

Stanier 5MTs 42964 and 42945 are alongside WD 2–8–0 90242 at Mold Junction, where all three locos were based on 14 September 1956. Maurice Dart/Transport Treasury.

On 5 September 1956 a stranger at Crewe station was Ivatt 2MT Mogul 46414 from Bury shed. Maurice Dart/Transport Treasury.

Several locos are lined up inside Bolton shed on 1 April 1956. Nearest is Ivatt 4MT 2–6–0 43018 from Leicester Midland shed which was ex Horwich Works. Behind it is 8F 2–8–0 48202 from Normanton shed. Behind that loco is Bolton's L & Y 0–6–0ST 51486. Maurice Dart.

A line of locos at Chester Northgate shed on 14 September 1956 included BR 2MT 2–6–0 78056 which had been recently allocated to the shed. Maurice Dart/Transport Treasury.

11

0–6–2 TANKS

GWR locos may have worked to Chester but photos of these have eluded me. Ex North Staffordshire Railway locos were sold to collieries by the LMS and were to be found operating in Lancashire. LNER locos worked in both counties.

The repair shops and main loco shed of the Manchester Collieries railway system was at Walkden near Tyldesley. I visited here informally on several occasions and was always permitted to have a look around. On 27 October 1957 ex NSR 'KING GEORGE VI' which had been LMS 2257 was outside the loco shed. The shed was usually referred to as 'Ellesmere loco shed' as it was adjacent to the closed Ellesmere colliery. Maurice Dart/Transport Treasury.

When I was approaching Walkden Yard on a push bike on 27 October 1957 I heard a train approaching and I turned off towards a railway embankment. Shortly ex NSR 'KENNETH' which had been LMS 2264 appeared hauling a short train and I obtained this shot of the loco on the skyline. Halfway down the embankment a line is descending from the right. Maurice Dart.

I watched and then approached the embankment and waited. I was rewarded when, after performing some shunting, 'KENNETH' descended the line to the lower level sandwiched between wagons. To the engine's left is an LMS 12T van. Maurice Dart/Transport Treasury.

In the early 1950s ex NSR 'PRINCESS' which was ex LMS 2271 is shunting alongside Ellesmere loco shed. This loco has a painted name whereas those in previous photos carried nameplates. In 1960 this loco went to Crewe Works where it was repainted in North Staffordshire Railway livery after which it took part in the NSR Centenary Exhibition at Stoke. In 1964 at Walkden Yard workshops it exchanged frames with ex NSR 'SIR ROBERT'. This loco which is preserved at the North Staffordshire Railway Centre at Cheddleton is coupled to Private Owner wagon SC 09322. Behind wagons outside the loco shed is 0–6–0ST 'JAMES' (RSH 7175/1944). Kenneth Brown.

We end this section with couple of shots of LNER locos. Locally based rather scruffy N5 class 69293 is at home at Chester Northgate shed on 16 September 1955. The number on the bunker side is hardly readable. Maurice Dart/Transport Treasury.

On 13 June 1949 N5/1 class 69361 heads a westbound goods past Cornbrook Junction as it approaches Trafford Park where the loco was allocated.

12

LMS, MIDLAND & L & Y 0–6–0s

Various classes of these locos worked Goods services in both counties.

We start this large section with two engines at their home shed at Dallam, Warrington on 12 September 1956. Nearest is 4F 0–6–0 44237 behind which is 8F 2–8–0 48520. Maurice Dart/Transport Treasury.

Next we have ex Midland Railway 2F 58128 at home at Newton Heath shed on 7 September 1956. The tender has been well filled with coal. Maurice Dart/ Transport Treasury

Now we start a large selection of views of the L & Y class 27 0–6–0s. Two local engines at home at Springs Branch shed on 29 September 1953 are 52143 which is head on to G2a class 0–8–0 49018. The 0–6–0's tender is not fitted with coal rails. Maurice Dart.

On 5 September 1956 52207 is coupled to LNER unfitted 6 plank open wagon E239326 at Crewe Works where the engine was based. The tender coupled to this engine is fitted with coal rails. Several of the class were based at Crewe Works at this time for use as works pilots. Maurice Dart/Transport Treasury.

A line of engines on shed at Bolton on 8 September 1955 are, from the left, 2P 4–4–0 40682, 0–6–0 52237 from Bury shed and 2–4–2T 50855. The first and third were local engines. Maurice Dart/ Transport Treasury.

On murky wet 11 September 1956 52240 is backing out of the yard at Blackpool North shed. This loco was allocated to Blackpool Central to which the North depot was a sub-shed. There are no coal rails on the tender. Maurice Dart/Transport Treasury.

Two local engines at home at Lees shed on 7 September 1956 are class 27 52248 which is being oiled by its driver and Fairburn 4MT 2–6–4T 42115. Maurice Dart/Transport Treasury.

Lees shed on 7 September 1956 contained another variation of the class 27 0–6–0s. Nearest is 52293 which has no coal rails on its tender but has been rebuilt with a boiler fitted with a Belpaire firebox. To its rear is Standard 2MT 2–6–2T 84013. Both engines were at their home shed. Maurice Dart.

Locally based 52389 is at Bolton shed on 1 April 1956. Visible to its left is the bunker of local Stanier 4MT 2–6–4 T 42633. On its right is the front of 8F 2–8–0 48678 from Wellingborough shed. Maurice Dart.

On 9 September 1956 52393 was at home at Springs Branch shed. Maurice Dart.

This is Lees shed late afternoon on 7 September 1956 full of locally based engines. On the left is Standard 2MT 2–6–2T 84019. Centre is class 27 52410 behind which is fellow class member 52293. Partly visible between locos is Stanier 2–6–4T 42115. On the right is the front of 52248. Maurice Dart/Transport Treasury.

On 29 September 1953 52449 was at home at Springs Branch shed. Maurice Dart.

In dire weather on 7 September 1956 I became well and truly waterlogged. As I had obtained shed permits and was using a circular tour book of 26 tickets, to avoid wastage I felt bound to stick to the planned timetable. Two engines stand at home in pouring rain outside Newton Heath shed mid-morning. They are Stanier 4MT 2–6–4T 42618 and 0–6–0 52455. Maurice Dart.

On 5 September 1956, 52459, another of the class 27s based at Crewe Works as pilots potters around as most enthusiasts in a visiting group pass it by simply noting its number. Maurice Dart/Transport Treasury.

Another of the class 27s which was allocated to Crewe Works was on shed at Bolton on 1 April 1956. Judging by its appearance 52464 has come to be 'run in' following an overhaul at Horwich Works. Maurice Dart/Transport Treasury.

11 September 1956 was another dire day of incessant hard rain. Outside Blackpool Central shed late morning is locally based 52466 which has a thin valance below the footplate and running plate providing yet another variation in design. On its left is Crab 2–6–0 42942 from Buxton shed. Maurice Dart.

This section ends with Blackpool Central's 52523 at Blackpool North shed on 11 September 1956. This provides yet another variation as the loco is 'saturated' and had been fitted with a Schmidt Superheater. On the right part of BR standard 16T Mineral wagon B 172155 is visible. Maurice Dart/Transport Treasury.

13
LNER 0–6–0s

These types operated goods trains in both counties. Every shot in this section depicts a J10 class loco.

We commence with a shot of J10/2 class 5644 at Wigan CLC shed on 1 July 1934. This loco was never re-numbered as it was withdrawn during June 1938. The small shed was situated at Lower Ince. I passed it several times after it had closed when walking to and from Springs Branch. When the shed closed on 24 March 1952 staff and locos were transferred to Springs Branch. Stephenson Locomotive Society.

This is Springs Branch shed on 9 September 1956 with four locally-based engines at home. On the right is Black Five 4–6–0 45026 which is carrying a 10A (Springs Branch) shed plate although official records show it as allocated to 10C (Patricroft). The three 0–6–0s on the left are J10/6 65176, J10/4 65131 and j10/6 65159. Maurice Dart.

In August 1958 J10/4 65140 is at home at Springs Branch shed. P. H. Groom.

Two engines at home at Chester Northgate shed on 14 September 1956 are 10/4 65143 and N5 class 0–6–2T 69293. Maurice Dart/Transport Treasury.

Also at home at Chester Northgate shed on 14 September 1956 was J10/4 65146. Maurice Dart/Transport Treasury.

On 29 September 1953 10/4 65148 is at home outside Springs Branch shed. To its right is the front of Jubilee class 4–6–0 45604 'CEYLON' from Crewe North shed. Maurice Dart/Transport Treasury.

At Lower Ince (Wigan CLC) shed on 24 April 1949 is locally based J10/4 65173. B. K. B. Green/Initial Photographics.

Springs Branch shed held local engines J10/6 65176 and J10/4 65131 on 9 September 1956. Maurice Dart.

On 16 September 1955 J10/6 65202 was at home among piles of ash at Northwich shed. The steam around the loco added a little atmosphere. Maurice Dart.

On 14 September 1956 Chester Northgate's J10/6 65208 was at home simmering in the yard. Maurice Dart.

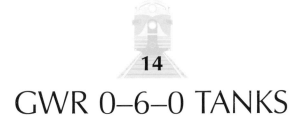

14

GWR 0–6–0 TANKS

These were to be found operating over the GWR lines in Cheshire.

Chester's 5700 class Pannier 5723 was moving around the yard at its home shed on 14 September 1956. Maurice Dart/Transport Treasury.

On 26 August 1962 Springs Branch shed had a most unusual visitor in the shape of GWR 5700 class Pannier 7762 which had been withdrawn from Stourbridge shed on 19 May. This loco which was en route to a scrapyard was very familiar to me as it was allocated to Laira shed for many years. Keeping it company was locally based G2A class 0–8–0 49008.

In the early 1960s 8750 class Pannier 3626 from Wellington shed enters Crewe with a local Passenger train which has run via Market Drayton.

Now we some of the older types of Pannier tank locos starting with 2021 class 2067 which is shunting at Birkenhead Docks in 1938. Note the bell which is fitted to the engine for use when approaching road crossings within the docks complex. A. C. Roberts/Real Photographs.

2021 class 2069 keeps 5101 class 4120 company at home at Birkenhead shed in September 1956. P. H. Groom.

To ease the workload at Swindon some GWR Pannier tanks were overhauled at Derby and at Crewe. On 6 February 1949 ex-Works 2021 class 2111 from Carmarthen shed keeps company with Holbeck shed's Royal Scot class 46117 'WELSH GUARDSMAN' outside Crewe Works. Also in the photo is Shrewsbury shed's Black Five 4–6–0 45318. T. J. Edgington.

Also fitted with a warning bell, Birkenhead shed's 1901 class half cab 2008 is at home in September 1956. P. H. Groom.

On the same day in September 1956 locally based, but not fitted with a bell, 1901 class 2012 was also on shed at Birkenhead. P. H. Groom.

15

LMS AND LNWR 0–6–0 TANKS

LMS Jintys worked in both counties as did LNWR tanks.

We start this short section with Sutton Oak's Jinty 47376 shunting on the Goods lines by St Helens Junction No.2 Signal Box on 22 August 1960. This was a quick 'grab shot' which I took from a passing train. Maurice Dart/Transport Treasury.

On 30 August 1952 Alsager's Jinty 47616 was simmering in the yard at its home shed. In the right background Stanier 4MT 2–6–4T 42447 is at the coal stage. In the background on the left is Ministry of Transport 16T unfitted mineral wagon MOT 19709 which was most probably in Bauxite livery. Maurice Dart/Transport Treasury.

On 16 March 1918 a train departed from Little Hulton Colliery sidings heading for Bolton Great Moor Street hauled by an LNWR 'Special' 0–6–0ST. Between 11 and 12 o'clock at night as the train descended towards Bolton the engine's brake power proved to be insufficient to control the loaded train and it gathered speed. As the train was diverted by a signalman into Crook Street yard the driver and fireman jumped clear. Despite a now slightly rising gradient the train continued and crashed through the buffer stops demolishing them. The engine continued across the yard running on cobbles and smashed through the boundary wall into Crook Street. It then entered one of the terraced houses where it dropped through the floor into the cellar. Amazingly no one was injured. This photo was probably taken the following day as a hawser has been attached to the loco to drag it out. F. D. Smith/J. A. Peden.

16

L & Y 0–6–0 TANKS

These were to be found working throughout the ex L & Y system. Also as with the class 27 0–6–0s a few were used as pilot locos at Crewe Works. These were built originally by Barton Wright as 0–6–0 tender locos. So in the captions where I state 'built by' this actually means 'rebuilt by'.

This large section consists mainly of shots of variations of class 23 Saddle tanks. At Aintree shed on 27 August 1952 is 51343 which was built by Kitson and was fitted with a Steam Brake. In the left background is Ivatt 2MT 2–6–2T 41284. Both were Aintree engines. Maurice Dart.

In LMS days 11375 receives some attention at Bank Hall shed.

On that very wet 7 September 1956 51381 is at home at Newton Heath shed. Built by Kitson this loco was fitted with a vacuum brake. Maurice Dart.

Two locally based engines alongside Accrington shed on 1 October 1953 are 51390 and Black Five 4–6–0 45225. The saddle tank was built by Beyer-Peacock and was fitted with a vacuum brake. Maurice Dart.

A few of the class 23 locos were used as pilot locos at Horwich and those retained their LMS numbers in the BR period. At the Works alongside Electric units on 14 September 1955 is 11394 which was built by Kitson and was fitted with a vacuum brake. Maurice Dart/Transport Treasury.

One of the Crewe Works pilot locos on 5 September 1956 was 51412. Beyer-Peacock built this loco which possessed a vacuum brake. The engine is shunting Crewe Works internal user 4 plank open wagon 021236. Maurice Dart.

Another of the pilot locos at Crewe Works on 5 September 1956 was 51446. This was built by Beyer-Peacock and had a vacuum brake. Maurice Dart/Transport Treasury.

Class 23 11456 was sold by the LMS to Coppull Colliery in 1937. On 7 May 1967 I walked along the NCB track from a level crossing over a public road to gain access to the yard at Parsonage Colliery, having been refused entry when I called at the offices a few days previously. I found my 'prize', 11456, which was devoid of any identification apart from an oval builder's plate. It was keeping company with a pair of unidentified 0–6–0 diesel shunters built by the Yorkshire Engine Co. 11456 is preserved on the Keighley & Worth Valley Railway and took part in the Rainhill celebrations held in 1980. Maurice Dart.

Outside Wigan Central L & Y shed on wet 29 September 1953 is locally based 51474. At the shed office the foreman denied me access but a while later I found a back lane which passed the shed yard and there was a very convenient large gap in the fence through which I quickly popped to record this engine. Built by Kitson it was fitted with a steam brake. The shed's 2P 4–4–0 40588 is alongside. Maurice Dart.

Withdrawn from Fleetwood shed, 51477 was being cut up at Horwich Works on 14 September 1955. Built by Kitson this loco had an automatic vacuum brake. Maurice Dart/Transport Treasury.

A pair of locos inside Bolton shed on 1 April 1956 are local class 23 51486 and 8F 2–8–0 48202 from Normanton shed. The saddle tank was built by the Vulcan Foundry and was fitted with an automatic vacuum brake. Maurice Dart.

On 30 March 1959 the same engine, 51486 waits at Bolton Trinity Street to proceed eastwards with a local goods.
Maurice Dart/Transport Treasury.

We end this section with a shot of one of the L & Y class 24 'dock tanks'. Partly cut up alongside the main shop at Horwich Works on 6 September 1956 is 51535 which had been withdrawn from Aintree shed. The loco retains its original 'block' buffers. Maurice Dart.

17
LNER 0–6–0 TANKS

Examples of these types worked in both counties but I possess very few photos of them.

Locos outside Gorton Works in 1948 are J10/4 0–6–0 5179 from Trafford park shed and J60 class 0–6–0T 8366 which had been withdrawn from Wrexham Rhosddu shed in March of that year.

J62 class saddle tank E8200 is outside Gorton Works where it has received an overhaul early in 1948. The E prefix denoted an Eastern Region loco. The loco was re-numbered to 68200 in June 1949. This loco which was based at Wrexham Rhosddu was withdrawn in November 1951.

J94 saddle tank 68063 is at home at Bidston shed on 26 August 1952. To its rear is O4/1 class 2–8–0 63722 from Gorton shed. Maurice Dart/Transport Treasury.

18

LNER 4–4–2 TANKS

These locos worked Passenger trains in both counties.

On 4 August 1955 Gorton's C13 class 67417 is entering Manchester London Road with a local working.

Gorton shed's C13 class 9009 (which became 7421 and then 67421) waits to depart from Guide Bridge with a train for Manchester London Road on 15 September 1945.

Outside Chester Northgate shed on 16 September 1955 are C13 class 67430 from Wrexham Rhosddu shed and locally based Ivatt 2MT 2–6–2T 41215. Maurice Dart/Transport Treasury.

At home at Chester Northgate shed on 16 September 1955 is C13 class 67436. Maurice Dart/ Transport Treasury.

On 6 August 1954 Gorton's C14 class 67448 waits to depart from Manchester London Road on a local Passenger working. Coupled to the loco is a virtually brand new BR standard non-corridor third class carriage.

19

GWR 4–4–0s

These locos worked in Cheshire and at times reached Manchester running via Warrington Bank Quay.

A visitor to Patricroft shed on 10 September 1938 was GWR Duke class 3268 'CHOUGH' from Oswestry shed. It had doubled headed a special 'Railway Carnival' train from Aberystwyth to Manchester Exchange with Dukedog 3211 'EARL OF DUCIE' which also based at Oswestry. To its rear is an ex LNWR 6F 0–8–2T.

In 1936 newly built 3203 'EARL CAWDOR' from Oswestry shed waits to depart from Crewe on a westbound passenger working. Officially called the Earl class these engines, which were nicknamed 'Dukedogs', were Swindon Hybrids built using the frames of Bulldog class 4–4–0s carrying boilers from Duke class 4–4–0s. The names were soon transferred to newly built Castle class 4–6–0s. A. G. Ellis collection.

Newly built Dukedog 3212 'EARL OF ELDON' which was an Oswestry engine awaits departure from Manchester Exchange with the 1.50pm train to Chester and North Wales during May 1937. W. Potter.

Another special 'Railway Carnival' train from Aberystwyth to Manchester Exchange on 10 September 1938 was worked by Dukedogs 3216 and 3212 'EARL OF ELDON' which were both Oswestry engines. 3216 is on the turntable at Patricroft shed after arrival.

20

LMS 4–4–0s

A large variety of these types operated trains in both counties.

I used to spend holidays at Westhoughton with friends from Plymouth who had returned home to Lancashire. I had read about Chequerbent incline which contained sections as steep as 1-in-27 and had photographed the closed station with an 0–8–0 shunting on a previous visit. This was on the line from Leigh to Bolton Great Moor Street. As there was only sparse traffic on the line I decided that the only way to see and obtain some photos of the incline was to unofficially walk down and back up it along the track. So on 4 September 1956 I cycled to Chequerbent station, where I left the bicycle, climbed through the wire strand fence and set off on the track down the bank. I had only gone a few yards when I heard a whistle of a train approaching behind me. I climbed up the low bank, opened my camera and turned around. 2P 40450 from Patricroft shed drifted past me as shown in this photo hauling one ex LMS Brake van containing track workers, guards and other railwaymen. I do not know who was most surprised, them or myself! I followed it down the bank and as I walked back up I took a couple of shots showing the uneven steep sections of the line. But my bonus was obtaining this unexpected shot. The track can be seen falling away beyond the overline bridge. Maurice Dart/Transport Treasury.

On 16 September 1955 a mid-morning train to Chester Northgate waits to depart from Manchester Central hauled by 2P 40559 from Llandudno Junction shed. Maurice Dart/Transport Treasury.

Bolton sheds 2P 40585 approaches Westhoughton on a local passenger train from Bolton on 6 September 1955. Maurice Dart.

Four engines can be seen at Chester Northgate shed on 16 September 1955. From the left they are local C13 class 4–4–2T 67436 and Ivatt 2MT 2–6–2T 41215. Next are 2P 4–4–0 40589 from Rhyl shed and locally based N5 0–6–2T 69293. Maurice Dart/Transport Treasury.

A pair of 2Ps in store at home at Chester LMS shed on 14 September 1956 are 40675 and 40679. Maurice Dart.

Locally based engines in store at Bolton shed on 8 September 1955 are L & Y 2P 2–4–2T 50647 and 2P 40682. Maurice Dart/Transport Treasury.

In the early 1920s Deeley MR 4P 993 is on a train at what appears to be Manchester Central. In 1927 this engine was re-numbered to 803 and was withdrawn the following year.

This is an exception as I do not normally include shots of the preservation era. Preserved 4P Midland Compound 1000 is in the yard at Manchester Liverpool Road on 22 August 1980. R. J. Buckley.

Two officials who could well be Locomotive Inspectors pose alongside LNWR Precursor class 2585 'WATT' at Crewe, north of the station in pre-grouping days. The loco has been converted to burn oil fuel. The loco was later re-numbered to 5236.

21

LNER 4–4–0s

These were to be found operating Passenger trains in both counties.

This is a pre-grouping shot of a Great Central Railway express from Manchester to Cleethorpes near Godley Junction. The train is double-headed and the pilot loco is D6 class 4–4–0 881 which became 5881 in July 1926. Withdrawal was during December 1932. The train engine is B4 class 4–6–0 1102 which became 6102 in February 1925. In 1947 it was supposed to be re-numbered to 1497 but it never carried that number and became 1487 in January 1947. This engine was withdrawn during December 1947. Railway Photographs.

D9 class 2304 from Brunswick shed, Liverpool pulls out of Manchester Central on 23 April 1947. Withdrawal was in January 1950.

D9 2305 from Northwich shed awaits departure from Manchester Central with a train to Chester Northgate on 14 June 1949. This loco was withdrawn in July 1950. Stanier 3MT 2–6–2T 86 from Uttoxeter shed is on the right.

At Gorton Works on 12 March 1948 D9 2313 from Trafford Park shed is keeping company with B9 class 4–6–0 1471. This 4–6–0 had been withdrawn from Heaton Mersey shed during October 1947 and has been partly cut up. The D9 survived until October 1949.

At home at Trafford Park shed on 13 June 1949 is D9 class 62317 which was withdrawn during July 1949. One section of this large shed was used by LMS locos.

One of the few named D9 class locos, 5104 'QUEEN ALEXANDRA' is on the turntable at Manchester Central in April 1936. this loco would have become 2326 but it was withdrawn in September 1944 before re-numbering took place.

D10 Director class 62653 'SIR EDWARD FRASER' is at home under the sheerlegs at Northwich shed on 16 September 1955. This engine was withdrawn three weeks later. A very intense white fire was burning between the engine and myself which made selecting a good vantage point rather difficult. Maurice Dart/Transport Treasury.

Northwich shed's D9 62659 'WORSLEY TAYLOR' is entering Altrincham on a train from Manchester Central on 8 August 1953.

D11/1 Director class 62661 'GERALD POWYS DEW-HURST' is at home outside Northwich shed in the mid-1950s. Mike Daly.

Heaton Mersey shed's D11/1 class 62665 'MONS' waits to depart from Manchester Central in 1952. The front carriage M26680 is probably a Brake Third. J. C. Hillmer.

On 24 April 1947 D20 class 2101 (which became 2360 and 62360) from Northwich shed is backing out of Chester Northgate to visit the shed.

2–2–2–2 AND 2–4–2 TANKS

The tender locos worked in both counties but I do not possess many photos of them. The tank locos were mainly to be found in Lancashire although a few found their way to Cheshire.

Despite appearances this loco is not a 2–4–2 as the driving wheels are not coupled. It is LNWR Great Britain class 2–2–2–2 Compound 2054 'QUEEN EMPRESS'. Fitted with 7ft diameter driving wheels it was built in 1893. In that year it went to the USA and featured in the Chicago Exhibition at which it won a Gold medal for excellence of workmanship after which it hauled a LNWR train from Chicago to New York. It was specially painted white with the Royal Coat of Arms in honour of Queen Victoria's Diamond Jubilee in 1897. It was recorded at Crewe Works.

London & North Western Railway.

Now we come to a large selection of L & Y class 5 2P 2–4–2 tanks. When I first saw one of these locos at Bolton in September 1953 I was impressed by its design and set out to photograph as many of the class as I was able. A Railtour for the Railway Correspondence & Travel Society enters Bolton Great Moor Street on 26 July 1953 hauled by 50644 from Warrington Dallam shed. B. K. B. Green/Initial Photographics.

After arriving at Bolton Great Moor Street on 26 July 1953 50644 has run around the train and is ready to depart on the next stage of the tour. This loco which has a short bunker is not carrying a BR crest or any lettering. B. K. B. Green/Initial Photographics.

On 12 September 1956 50644 was at home at Dallam shed, Warrington. Maurice Dart/Transport Treasury.

One of the local engines in store with its chimney covered at Bolton shed on 8 September 1955 was 50647 which also has a short bunker. Maurice Dart/Transport Treasury.

The first of the class which I saw, 50650 was at home inside Bolton shed on 28 September 1953. This loco is fitted with a Belpaire boiler. Maurice Dart.

Belpaire boiler fitted 50651 was at home alongside Rose Grove shed on 1 October 1953. Maurice Dart/Transport Treasury.

Also at home at Rose Grove shed on 1 October 1953 was Belpaire boiler fitted 50652. Maurice Dart/Transport Treasury.

On very wet 10 September 1956 50660 from Lees shed brings a train of vans though Bolton Trinity Street. The leading vehicle is an ex MR 6-wheeled clerestory passenger train brake van. Maurice Dart.

On the dump at Horwich Works awaiting cutting up on 14 September 1955 was Belpaire boiler fitted 50686 which had been withdrawn from Manningham shed four days earlier. Maurice Dart/Transport Treasury.

In the 1930s 10695 from Wakefield shed is on the turntable at Bank Hall shed, Liverpool.

Two of the class are at home inside Warrington Dallam shed on 12 September 1956. At the back of the shed is 50643 and nearest to the camera is 50705. Maurice Dart.

Cutting up had commenced on 50714 at Horwich Works on 30 September 1953. This loco which had been withdrawn from Manningham shed was still lettered LMS. Maurice Dart.

On snowy 3 January 1952 50731 from Bury shed waits to depart from Holcombe Brook with the branch Motor train which it will propel to Bury Bolton Street. This branch line closed a few months later in May. N. R. Knight.

For my two-week holiday in these two counties in September 1956 I had obtained permits for most of the sheds I wished to visit. The exceptions were Wigan L & Y where the Foreman denied me access, and Southport. So on 4 September 1956 after failing to go around Wigan shed I headed for Southport where, after talking to the foreman for several minutes I was given permission to have a look around. At the top end of the yard, waiting to go off shed was locally based 50746. In the left background Bolton's Stanier 4P 2–6–4T 42545 is outside the shed. Maurice Dart.

On 2 January 1960 Bolton shed's 50850 with a Belpaire boiler approaches Blackrod with the 12.13pm Horwich to Bolton Trinity Street train. Transport Treasury.

Two local engines in store at Bolton shed on 8 September 1955 are 3F 0–6–0 52237 and 50855 which is fitted with a large bunker. Maurice Dart/Transport Treasury.

This section ends with LNER F2 class 5783 (which became 7111) at Trafford Park shed in June 1934. This loco was withdrawn in December 1950.

23

LMS 0–4–4 TANKS

These Barton Wright L & Y engines were withdrawn from service between roughly 1900 and 1916. However some of them saw further use for many years as carriage warmers at a number of locations in the ex L & Y area. They were usually tucked away in odd corners at large stations or hidden behind rolling stock in carriage sidings. These locos had their motion and driving wheels removed and most lost all form of identification. Also some locos were replaced by a different class member. Many hours have been spent researching the class to attempt to identify these locos without much success. Where known I have quoted possible numbers. These locos were fitted with tall extensions to their chimneys which would not fit in most photographs.

This is stated to be definitely 713 at Accrington in 1954. However, when I visited Accrington shed in October 1953 I did not see this loco. Perhaps it was in a siding remote from the shed.

When I was on the 1956 two week holiday I knew there were reputed to be a couple of these locos at Blackpool Central. On arrival I looked around the station to no avail and after visiting the two sheds I did a trip to Fleetwood from Blackpool North. A loco of this type was reputed to be at the North station but I did not find it. After this I returned to Blackpool Central and after a good search around I located two of the class on the east side of the station. They had previously been obscured by parked carriages. Here are the two locos on 11 September 1956, one of which is 910. Maurice Dart/Transport Treasury.

Here are the same pair of locos, one of which is 910 at Blackpool Central on 27 August 1957. The photographer was standing outside the public area to obtain this photo. M . J. Jackson.

Also on 27 August 1957 another member of the class was at Blackpool North station. I did not see this loco at this location in September 1956. M. J. Jackson.

The Locomotive Inspector who lived next door to my friend at Moseley Hill, Liverpool, arranged a few visits for me. Most were to loco sheds but one was to the area south of Edge Hill on the original route which ran to Crown Street and the Wapping tunnel. He had told me that he was going to show me an old engine and as we descended steps to Edge Hill Carriage sidings I espied this 0–4–4T at the back of a building across several tracks. In his company on 17 August 1966 I was able to approach it and took this photo. Despite scouring it completely I was unable to find any identification. From there we walked the line to Crown Street through each tunnel and walked halfway down the Wapping tunnel until darkness prevented us exploring further. Maurice Dart.

There were two of the class at Horwich Works on 6 September 1956. One was inside the repair shop and was not photographable. Here is the other which examination showed to be 913. This engine had been withdrawn from service in 1918. To its right is 'Austln Seven' 0–8–0 49552 which had been withdrawn from Newton Heath shed. Maurice Dart/Transport Treasury.

Here is one of the class actually carrying the number 926 at Horwich Works on an unknown date. When was the photo taken? Where had the engine arrived from and where was it destined to go?

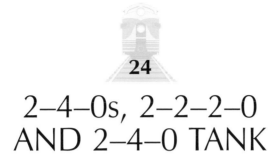

24

2–4–0s, 2–2–2–0 AND 2–4–0 TANK

2–4–0s were to be found operating in both counties as were 2–2–2–0s. I have only seen photos of 2–4–0Ts working in Cheshire.

We start this section of old locos with GWR 'Stella' class 2–4–0 3201 at Chester station, probably in the late 1920s. This engine was built by the GWR at Swindon in December 1884 but was sold to the Pembroke & Tenby Railway in January 1885 when brand new. It became their No.8 and was given the name 'STELLA' which it carried on an oblong plate on the cabside. It became GWR property again in 1896 and carried its name until 1902. Later it was reboilered and other modifications were carried out. Many of the class ended their days at Chester and Croes Newydd sheds. This engine worked until October 1933.

Now we have LNWR 6' 'Jumbo' class 2–4–0 'ENGINEER CREWE' at Crewe South shed, probably in the 1920s. Originally this engine was numbered 209 and was named 'PETREL'. Real Photographs Co. Ltd.

LNWR 6' 'Jumbo' class 2–4–0 414 'PROSPERRO' at the south end of Crewe station in the early 1900s. Jerome Ltd.

LNWR 6'7½" 'Precedent' class 2–4–0 'HARDWICKE' is at Crewe Works on an unknown date. This loco which became LMS 5031 made a record run during the railway race to Aberdeen. On 22 August 1895 whilst working the 8pm express from Euston it ran between Crewe and Carlisle at an average sped of 67.2 MPH. This engine, which was built in 1873 is preserved and forms part of the National collection. London & North Western Railway Company.

LNWR 6'7½" 'Precedent' class 2–4–0 955 'CHARLES DICKENS' stands outside Crewe Works with a goodly group of older generation railwaymen on an unknown date. Pamlin Prints.

Here is LNWR 2–2–2–0 1306 'IONIC' at Crewe Works. This was one of the final batch of locos of this wheel arrangement and was built in 1890. On 8 September 1895 this engine worked a train non-stop over the 299 miles from Euston to Carlisle at an average speed of 51 MPH. Note the track of the Crewe Works internal 18" gauge railway system, the first section of which opened in 1862. London & North Western Railway Company.

This unusual section ends with GWR experimental 2–4–0T No.1 at Chester, probably in the 1920s. This engine was built in May 1880 as a 4–4–0T and was rebuilt as a 2–4–0T in May 1882. It remained in service until July 1924 when it was withdrawn from Wellington shed. Apparently because of its uniqueness and number it was much sought after by railway enthusiasts. Locomotive & General Railway Photographs.

25

0–4–2 TANK AND LMS 0–4–0 TANKS

This section contains a sole 0–4–2T in Cheshire but LNWR locos probably worked in Lancashire. Various examples of LMS 0–4–0Ts were to be found operating in both counties.

We start with GWR 3571 class 0–4–2T 3573 at home on the ash pits at Birkenhead shed in July 1937 alongside a GWR Loco Coal wagon. This engine had moved to Worcester by March 1938 and was withdrawn from Swindon shed in December 1945. Rex Conway collection.

A pair of Sentinel shunters are at Sutton Oak shed, St Helens on 26 April 1951. Strictly speaking these vertical boilered locos are not 0–4–0Ts as their wheels are not coupled and are usually described as 4wVBGTs. They are included in this section for convenience. Both 47180 and 47184 were allocated here and would have worked over sharply curved sidings which served industrial premises in the area. Built in 1930 and 1931 they were numbered 7160 and 7164 until 1939. 47184 is a smaller 'industrial' type loco which the LMS purchased for use at Clee Hill Quarries in Shropshire. Two private owner wagons are to the rear of the locos. H.C.Casserley.

Here is LMS 0F shunter 1541 at Crewe and the wall behind the loco suggests it is at the North shed. It was built in 1930 and in 1934 was renumbered to 7001.

This is the same loco, by now numbered 47001 and allocated to Bank Hall shed. It is shunting BR Standard 16T vacuum braked mineral wagons at Alexandra Dock goods yard on 28 August 1959. That day I had obtained permission to visit the railway system of the Mersey Docks & Harbour Board and set off northwards from the head offices walking along the docks looking for locos and their sheds. After leaving Canada Dock shed I saw smoke outside the dock wall and heard whistling so I exited through one of the gates and across the road was the large entrance to this goods yard. Two locos were in the yard so I ventured along the perimeter road towards them. As I approached them the shunters saw me, waved me over and posed against the loco as I took my photo. The other loco, a Jinty 0–6–0T set off from the far side of the yard with a train as I took this shot and eluded the camera. Maurice Dart/Transport Treasury.

On 17 June 1934 another of the class, 1542 (later 7002) is outside Edge Hill shed where it was probably allocated, although the shed plate is unreadable. As this engine is in a rather dirty condition I hazard a guess that it has been running through the long tunnel to work at Wapping Dock recently.

Now we come to a large batch of the small L & Y Rly 0F 'Pugs'. I first saw one of these locos, 11212 far away from its home, inside Barrow Road shed, Bristol in August 1946 and I developed a fascination for the class. I tried to see as many as possible but most were usually inside sheds. I was aware that many worked at the dock's goods yards in Liverpool so one evening in September 1952, assuming that most would have returned to shed I visited Bank Hall shed around 8.30pm. I passed the offices and descended the steps and met the Running Foreman outside his office. He was most surprised to find an enthusiast entering in the dark. We had a chat and he told me that the Shedmaster had no time for 'Engine Spotters' but tolerated genuine enthusiasts. I explained my interest in 'Pugs' and he confirmed that all had returned to shed. He told me to write down all of the locos I could see and put my notebook away before the Shedmaster came along. He introduced me to said gentleman who, after a long chat about locos personally took me around the shed. He told me not to write any numbers down but impressed on me any locos which were 'missing'. So I saw all of the allocated 'Pugs', 0–6–0 'Dock and Saddle Tanks'. I have collected photos of them to compensate for my lack of opportunities. The locos are all at their home sheds or areas. This is a 'desperate' shot which I took of 51204 inside the confines of Widnes shed on 12 September 1956. I rested the camera on a bench to carry out a time exposure but I was unable to include all of the loco from that angle, but 'beggars cannot be choosers' as we say in Plymouth. At the top left the funnel and boiler top of LNER J10/4 0–6–0 65138 which was a Widnes engine can be seen. Maurice Dart/Transport Treasury.

Pug 51206 carrying the shed code 23A is moving around the yard at Bank Hall shed in the 1950s. Stephenson Locomotive Society.

This is grubby 11214 at Horwich Works in company with another member of the class, probably following withdrawal which occurred before 1934.

In the 1950s 51230 is at Agecroft shed where it was allocated for many years.
Stanley J. Rhodes.

In the mid-1940s 11231 is at Bank Hall shed. Several other members of the class are in the background.
Stanley J. Rhodes.

In 1949 51237 was outside one of the two sheds at Bank Hall. Stephenson Locomotive Society.

Most unusually I have included a shot taken in the preservation era. Pug 11243 was sold out of service into industry by the LMS in the early 1931 when it was purchased by Contractors John Mowlem. Named 'BASSET' it was used on a contract to extend Southampton Docks. In 1935 it was sold to the United Glass Bottle Manufacturers who renamed it 'PRINCE'. Following preservation at the Keighley & Worth Valley Railway the loco moved to its present location on 31 March 1999. I recorded it at the Riversway site at Preston Docks during a visit by train by the Branch Line Society on 24 March 2007. Maurice Dart.

In the 1930s 11246 is at Lower Darwen shed in front of an L & Y R 0–6–0ST.

At Bank Hall shed outside the office block is 11248 which was withdrawn from service before 1934.

In 1949 at Bank Hall shed are Pug 11253 and Compound 41193 which was allocated there. Note the 'spark arrestor' disc which was fitted to most of these locos which were allocated to Bank Hall. Stephenson Locomotive Society.

The same loco, 51253 is resting from shunting in Alexandra Dock goods yard in the 1950s. In the background are several old grounded carriage bodies in use as offices.

26

SERVICE AND PRESERVED LOCOS, SHED SCENES AND ACCIDENT

Service or Departmental locos were to be found operating at loco, carriage and wagon works, Engineer's yards and depots and sometimes at loco sheds. The one preserved loco is at an LMS Works. The other categories are self-explanatory.

Ex LNWR Service loco, LMS 0–4–2 Crane Tank 3247 is at Crewe Works, probably in 1930s. There were eight of these shunters at various Works and this loco survived until 1946.
D.S.Barrie.

LNWR 'Bissel Truck' 0–4–2ST 47862 is at Crewe Works on 5 September 1956. Although numbered in Capital Stock it was one of two of the type which were based at the Works as Service locos for shunting.
Maurice Dart/Transport Treasury.

Next we see 0–4–0ST 'WREN' at Horwich Works, probably in the 1930s. This was one of the locos which worked on the internal 18" gauge railway which serviced areas of the Works. Normal 'works clutter' fills the area behind the loco. W. Leslie Good.

'WREN' is the subject of a group of enthusiasts who were visiting Horwich Works on 24 April 1949. B. K. B. Green/Initial Photographics.

On 10 June 1959 LMS 88 hp Fowler 0–4–0 Diesel Mechanical Departmental loco ED1 was outside Newton Heath shed. It is buffered up to BR standard unfitted mineral wagon B 150250. In the background is 8F 2–8–0 48745 which was allocated to the shed. Alec Swain/Transport Treasury.

On 1 October 1959 150 hp Fowler 0–4–0 Diesel Mechanical Departmental loco ED6 was in the yard at Castleton Permanent Way Depot coupled to a BR Standard Single Bolster wagon which had a 10ft wheelbase. Transport Treasury.

This is a preservation shot with a difference as it was taken in Horwich Works Paint Shop on 14 September 1955 which was way before the later preservation era commenced. Furness Railway 0–4–0 No. 3 'COPPERNOB' was on display at this location for many years. Maurice Dart/Transport Treasury.

We now come to a selection of scenes at loco sheds and commence at Trafford Park on 13 June 1949. This was a CLC shed with sections occupied by the LMS and LNER. This shows the LNER section. Several J10 class 0–6–0s have their tender's facing the camera but the two D9/2 class 4–4–0s are 62307 'QUEEN MARY' and un-named 62317.

To celebrate the Centenary of the Liverpool & Manchester Railway an exhibition was held at Manchester Victoria Station during September and October 1930. Locos from various railways attended and were held at sheds in the area on arrival. This unusual scene was recorded at Agecroft shed in September 1930. From the left the locos are L & Y 5P 4–6–0 10452, GWR 6029 'KING STEPHEN' (later re-named 'KING EDWARD VIII'), SR 4–6–0 850 'LORD NELSON' and Liverpool & Manchester Rly 0–4–2 'LION' which dates from 1838. A. G. Ellis.

This is the line up outside Bolton shed on 1 April 1956. From the left the locos are 4MT 2–6–4T 42545, L & Y 3F 0–6–0 52389, 4MT 2–6–4Ts 42654, 42655, 42630, 7F 0–8–0 49544 and WD 2–8–0 90641. All of these engines were allocated there. Maurice Dart/Transport Treasury.

At home standing beneath the automatic Coaling plant at Bolton shed on 8 September 1955 is 4MT 2–6–4T 42565. The ash plant is in the distance to the right.

Maurice Dart/Transport Treasury.

Three L & Y engines are at home in the depths at the back end of Bolton shed on 1 April 1956. From the left they are 3F 0- 6–0 52237 and 2–4–2Ts 50850 and 50855. This was a time exposure obtained by resting the camera on a nearby bench. Maurice Dart.

No date is quoted for this visit to Bury shed by a group of enthusiasts. From the left locos identifiable are Crab 42712, 4MT 2–6–4T 42460, Ivatt 2–6–0 46486, Crab 2–6–0s 42719, 42764 and Ivatt 2–6–0 46436. I have not quoted any allocations for these locos due to the date being unknown. The roof of the adjacent Electric Unit depot is on the right. A.Scarsbrook/Initial Photographics.

This is an undated shot of the north end of Bacup shed which was probably taken in the 1930s. Five L & Y locos are in yard. On the left a 3F 0–6–0 is in front of what appears to be a pair of 2–4–2Ts. Next to them is 3F 0–6–0 12124 which is the only loco identifiable. On the right is what appears to be an 0–8–0.

This is a shot taken inside the Old Works at Crewe on an unknown date. The two front locos are 0–8–0s 9430 and 9388 behind which appears to 9316. The third loco in the line is a named 4–6–0, probably a Prince Of Wales class. W. Leslie Good.

We end this section with a shot of the recovery operations following a disastrous derailment which occurred on 4 November 1924. L & Y 4–4–0 1405 was working a Liverpool Exchange to Blackpool express. Near Lytham the tyre on one of the wheels of the loco broke. The loco left the rails and crashed into a signal box. Two carriages were demolished and another caught fire. Fourteen passengers died in the accident.

27
LMS ELECTRIC SETS

These operated in both counties but I only have a few photos in my collection.

This is an undated shot of Mersey Railway No.4 at Birkenhead North depot. This was a 1st class motor bogie car which originally operated on the Liverpool Overhead Railway. A. R. Wilson.

This is a six car unidentified Mersey Railway train at an unidentified station which could possibly be Birkenhead North. Is any reader able to help with this conumdrum? John C. Gillham.

An ex-Midland Railway Electric train is departing from Morecambe for Heysham on an unknown date. The lines on the right lead to Lancaster.

28

ELECTRIC LOCOS

Variants of these were to be found operating in both counties.

We start this section with a few shots of 1300hp Bo-Bo EM1 class electric locos. In 1964 an express from Manchester Piccadilly crossing Broadbottom viaduct is hauled by B1 class 4–6–0 61360 which was a long way from home as it was allocated to Stratford shed. As it is very clean it may well be 'running in' following a visit to Gorton or Doncaster Works. The train is piloted by the original EM1 class loco 26000 'TOMMY' which was allocated to Reddish depot. Originally numbered 6701 and then 6000 it was built in February 1941 and was loaned to the Netherlands Railways for extensive trials from September 1947 until February 1952. Due to the Second World War construction of further members of the class did not re-commence until 1950.

A freight from the Manchester area passes Torside on 28 March 1978 hauled by EM1 class 76003 from Reddish depot. This loco had previously been numbered 26036 and 76036. John Scrace.

This undated photo has Reddish depot's EM1 class 26010 bringing a Manchester bound freight out of the west portal of the new Woodhead tunnel. The two original trackless single line bores are on the left. The photo pre-dates 21 February 1973 when this loco was renumbered to 76010.

EM1 class 26020 from Reddish depot stands at Manchester London Road on 13 August 1960. This station was re-named Manchester Piccadilly on 12 September that year. Maurice Dart/Transport Treasury.

Now we have a selection of electric locos which operated over the North Western routes and have an undated shot of 3200hp class 81 E3016 (later 81014) at Crewe. To the left is part of GWR 8750 class 0–6–0PT 9630 from Wellington shed which was working a service via Market Drayton. This would have been taken in the early 1960s when the EM1 class loco was based at either Crewe Electric depot or to AC Lines at either Crewe Electric or at Allerton. Frank Sperritt.

Crewe Electric depot's 3200hp class 81 81015 (ex E3017) waits at the north end of Preston station on 4 September 1973.

During an Open Day at Crewe Works on 22 September 1979 3300hp class 82 82005 (ex E3051) from Longsight depot was in the yard awaiting attention.

2950hp class 83 83008 (ex E3031) is at home on Longsight depot on 3 September 1973.

Crewe Electric depot based 3200hp class 85 85101 (ex 85006 and E3061) is in a line of locos at Crewe station in the early 1990s. This loco has been saved for preservation at Barrow Hill shed.

4040hp Longsight depot based 86226 (ex E3162) heads a northbound express at Wigan North Western on dismal 9 August 1997. In October 2009 this loco was stored at Long Marston depot. Maurice Dart.

Willesden based 5000hp class 87 87031 'HAL O'THE WYND' brings an express into Manchester Piccadilly in the 1990s. This loco was stored at Long Marston depot in October 2009.

On 10 August 1997 Willesden depot's 5000hp class 90 90001 has arrived at Manchester Piccadilly on a express from London. Maurice Dart.

SNCF owned 6760hp class 92 92014 'EMILE ZOLA' is stabled at the south end of Warrington Bank Quay on 4 March 2001. Late in 2009 this loco was stored at Crewe Electric depot. Maurice Dart.

29

DIESEL LOCOS

Various types of these locos operated throughout both counties.

We start with LMS 0–6–0 diesel 1831 outside the Paint Shop at Crewe Works on 21 August 1949. This little recorded loco may have started life as Midland Railway 1F 0–6–0T 1999, built in September 1892 which was renumbered to 1831 in November 1907. It has been postulated that the frames of that loco were used to build the diesel although the fact that the diesel loco's frames were 8″ longer than the original causes some doubt, but an extension may well have been inserted. Completed at Derby Works in November 1932 this 600hp Diesel hydraulic shunter worked mainly in the Derby area and at Toton until it was pit to store at Derby in November 1936. In January 1940 it was converted to a Mobile Power Generating Unit, numbered MPU3 and moved to Crewe Works for completion of the task. After working at Coventry, Crewe North shed and moving to Derby Works it arrived at Crewe Works carrying no identification as shown here. Following a period here and at Crewe South shed it was cut up at Crewe Works after September 1955. To its rear is ex Midland Railway 3 plank wagon 1808. R. S. Carpenter Photos.

Passing south through Crewe on 11 September 1990 a pair of 1000hp class 20 diesel electrics head an Engineer's train. Both based at Toton 20228 (ex D8128) is leading 20215 (ex D8315).

In mid-1973 1250hp class 25 diesel electric 25276 (ex D7626) based at Springs Branch brings a van train east through Manchester Victoria. The leading vehicle is an ex LMS Stanier Full Brake carriage.

Crewe Diesel based 1470hp class 31 diesel electric 31142 (ex D5560) stands at the south end of Crewe station on 10 September 1990.

On 15 April 1997 Crewe Diesel allocated 1750hp class 37 diesel electric 37414 'CATHAYS C & W WORKS 1846–1993' has arrived at Crewe on a train from Holyhead. This loco had previously been numbered 37287 and D6987. Maurice Dart.

In the mid-1990s Crewe diesel allocated 2750hp diesel electric 47806 (ex 47651, 47254, D1931) awaits departure from Manchester Piccadilly to run to Longsight depot.

In the late 1990s Cardiff Canton allocated 3250hp class 56 diesel electric 56103 'STORA' is coupled to another of the same type at Warrington Bank Quay. Following two periods working in France this loco was in store at Crewe Diesel depot late in 2009.

On 12 September 1990 Toton allocated 3300hp class 58 diesel electric 58042 'IRONBRIDGE POWER STATION' waits for the road at the south end of Crewe station. Late in 2009 this loco was operating in France.

Heavy freight 3250hp class 66 diesel electric locos see occasional use on passenger trains when used to haul railtours. On 24 March 2007 Toton allocated 66009 waits to depart from Manchester Victoria with a Branch Line Society Charter train which visited the Ribble Steam Railway at Preston Docks via the steeply graded branch line from south of Preston station. This was a line which I had not previously ridden over. Maurice Dart.

30

LIVERPOOL OVERHEAD RAILWAY AND INDUSTRIAL LOCOS

The heading to this section is self-explanatory.

Liverpool Overhead Railway three-car train No.13 on a southbound journey has stopped at James Street station probably in the early 1950s. John C. Gillham.

This interesting photo from the early 1950s has a three-car northbound Liverpool Overhead Railway train passing over a section of the Mersey Docks & Harbour Board Railway at one of the points where the lines exited the docks to cross the road to connect with one of the adjacent BR goods yards. It could be near Alexandra Dock Goods yard. MDHB 0–6–0ST 6 (HE 1827/1937) is stopped below 'The Dockers Umbrella' as the LOR was called locally.

The last photo leads into a selection of shots of MDHB locos, most of which I took during a visit which I made to the system on 28 August 1959. I obtained permission to visit the docks railway system for a days walk around and reported to Princes Dock loco shed offices at 10am. Some of the sheds were tucked away among the dock buildings and took a bit of searching out. I reached Hornby Dock late afternoon and time prevented me proceeding to Gladstone Dock. Instead I used a bus to head south to Brunswick Dock. To save repetition in this section I will only quote a date if it is different from that of my visit. We commence with MDHB 0–6–0ST 1 (AE 1465/1904) outside the east end of the shed at Canada Dock. Maurice Dart/Transport Treasury.

MDHB 0–6–0ST 2 (AE 1813/1918) was awaiting scrapping outside Princes Dock shed and repair shop. One of the front buffers has been removed. Maurice Dart/Transport Treasury.

MDHB 0–6–0ST 4 (AE 2006/1930) was partly outside the south end of Brunswick Dock shed. The loco has a small plate carrying a letter T affixed to the smokebox door the significance of which eludes me. Maurice Dart/Transport Treasury.

On 25 October 1947 MDHB 0–6–0ST 7 (AE 1523/1907) awaits repair at Princes Dock shed. Above the loco steps lead to the Liverpool Overhead Railway Princes Dock station. Kenneth Brown.

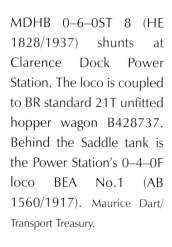

MDHB 0–6–0ST 8 (HE 1828/1937) shunts at Clarence Dock Power Station. The loco is coupled to BR standard 21T unfitted hopper wagon B428737. Behind the Saddle tank is the Power Station's 0–4–0F loco BEA No.1 (AB 1560/1917). Maurice Dart/ Transport Treasury.

MDHB 0–6–0ST 9 (HE 1984/1940) is under repair outside the north end of Princes Dock shed. Maurice Dart/Transport Treasury.

MDHB 0–6–0ST 10 (AE 1571/1910) is outside the east end of Canada Dock shed. Maurice Dart/Transport Treasury.

MDHB 0–6–0ST 11 (HE 1985/1940) has arrived at the west side of Huskisson Dock shed. In the right background are banana vans, the farthest one being ex SR. Maurice Dart/Transport Treasury.

Three MDHB 0–6–0STs are inside the large two road shed at Canada Dock. From the right they are 17 (AE 1619/1912), 21 (AE 1671/1913) and 14 (HE 1682/1931) which had previously worked at Haifa harbour. Outside the shed are previously shown 10 and 1. This well laid out shed was larger than many BR sub-sheds. Maurice Dart/Transport Treasury.

Very clean MDHB 0–6–0ST 24 (AE 1741/1916) stands alongside 0–6–0DM 32 (HE 2699/1944) outside Hornby Dock shed. Maurice Dart/Transport Treasury.

MDHB 0–6–0STs 25 (AE 1809/1918) and 16 (AE 1621/1912) are outside the south end of Brunswick Dock shed.
Maurice Dart/Transport Treasury.

Several locos were inside the cramped and gloomy Brunswick Dock shed. One under repair was MDHB 0–6–0ST 27 (AE 1811/1918). Maurice Dart.

This is the cramped two road shed at Huskisson Dock. Two MDHB 0–6–0STs inside were taking water in turn from a pipe hanging down from the upper parts of the shed. The stopcock for the tank was accessed by means of the ladder visible inside the entrance. On the left is 30 (HE 2079/1941) with 7 (AE 1523/1907) on the right. Maurice Dart.

MDHB 0–6–0DM 32 (HE 2699/1944) is outside Hornby Dock shed alongside 0–6–0ST 24 seen earlier. Maurice Dart/Transport Treasury.

Receiving attention outside the south end of Brunswick Dock shed is MDHB 0–6–0DM 35 (HC D1036/1958). This recently arrived loco had been fitted with a modified exhaust for working at Dingle Oil Jetty and was permanently allocated to Brunswick Dock shed. The inscription on the Cheshire Lines Railway offices at Brunswick goods station forms an interesting backdrop to this photo. Maurice Dart/Transport Treasury.

Another brand new loco, MDHB 0–6–0DM 37 (HC D1038/1958) is outside Hornby Dock shed. This shed in particular took me quite a bit of ferreting around to locate. The vast expanses of the docks which form a backdrop were most impressive to me. Maurice Dart/Transport Treasury.

Having reached Brunswick Dock shed by around 6pm I made my way onward to Dingle Oil Jetty which was officially 'off limits' to me according to my permit. However I took a chance and located the object of the exercise. MDHB 0–6–0F 43 (AE 1573/1918) was working on the jetty and the driver exchanged cordial greetings with me. The cliffs rise impressively behind the dockside buildings. Maurice Dart/Transport Treasury.

Clarence Dock Power Station, situated within the MDHB complex was also 'off limits' to me according to my permit. As an MDHB saddle tank was shunting inside the gate I took a chance and ventured in. 0–4–0F BEA No.1 (AB 1560/1917) was only a few yards inside. Maurice Dart/Transport Treasury.

I knew there was another loco present at Clarence Dock Power Station so I enquired its whereabouts and was directed to it. I found 0–4–0ST BEA No.2 (RSH 7646/1950) standing outside the power station's offices so I quickly took a photo and departed on my tramp north along the docks. Maurice Dart/Transport Treasury.

Next we have a selection of NCB owned locos. Whilst on holiday staying with friends at Westhoughton I occasionally borrowed one of their bicycles and using a 1″ OS map I attempted to visit some locations where locos were to be found. As these visits were always on the spur of the moment I never obtained any permits, but on only one occasion, in the 1970s at Parsonage colliery, was I ever refused admission. This section starts with 0–6–0T 'JOSEPH' (HE 1456/1924) at the Engineering workshop/ repair centre at Walkden

yard on 27 October 1957. The loco is standing next to BR standard 16T unfitted mineral wagon B140970. Maurice Dart/Transport Treasury.

Alongside one of the sheds at Walkden yard on 27 October 1957 is 0–4–0ST 'KING' (AB 1448/1919). To its right is private owner 13T 8 plank mineral wagon P20105. Maurice Dart/Transport Treasury.

On 27 October 1957 at the back end of one of the lines in the two road repair shop at Walkden yard was this gem. It is 0–6–0T 'T. B. WOOD' (Lowca 233/1899). Maurice Dart/ Transport Treasury.

Hidden away in a small compound between two of the buildings at Walkden yard on 27 October 1957 was 0–4–0ST 'OUTWOOD No. 1' (P 932 /1901) which was in use as a stationary boiler supplying steam to the repair shop. Maurice Dart/Transport Treasury.

Tucked away in the same compound at Walkden yard on 27 October 1957 was veteran 0–4–0ST 'PECKETT' (P518/1890). Maurice Dart/Transport Treasury.

Fresh from rebuilding 0–6–0ST 'WEASEL' (HE 3844/1957) was at work at Brackley colliery on 27 October 1957. Maurice Dart/Transport Treasury.

Standing near a servicing pit at Brackley colliery on 28 March 1959 is 0–6–0ST 'JAMES' (RSH 7175/1944). There was no loco shed at this location. Note the narrow gauge tub wagons on two different levels of the structures behind the loco. Maurice Dart/Transport Treasury.

Fitted with a Giesl ejector 0–6–0ST 'REPULSE' (HE 3698/1950) is working at Mosley Common colliery on 17 August 1966. Engines which worked here were based at Ellesmere shed, Walkden yard. Maurice Dart.

On 28 March 1959 a pair of locos were in a most un-photographable position between the loco shed at Astley Green colliery and a spoil bank. Nearest the camera is 0–6–0T 'FRANCIS' (KS 3068/1917). To its rear is much smaller 0–4–0ST 'CARR' (HC 1812/1948). This colliery has become the site of a Mining Museum. Maurice Dart.

On 27 October 1957 I visited the NCB Opencast Executive site at Peel Hall where after some intense questioning I was permitted to see the loco. Inside the small loco shed (a Nissen hut) at the outermost end of the site was ex WD 0–6–0ST 71499 (HC 1776/1944). Maurice Dart/ Transport Treasury.

On 28 March 1959 I found my way to Howe Bridge colliery near Platt bridge as I had read that an unusual elderly loco was still to be found there. To my sheer delight my 'prize' was out working so here is 0–4–0ST 'CRAWFORD' which had been built by the Wigan Coal & Iron Company in 1887. No works numbers were allocated. Maurice Dart/ Transport Treasury.

When I happen to be in just the right place at the right time by accident one of my fellow enthusiast friends uses an expression which is 'Dart jam'! This happened when I was on a train travelling from York to Liverpool Lime Street on 22 August 1960. Normally, if possible when on a train passing points of interest I would stand in the corridor by a partly open window with my camera open around my neck set ready for action. This paid off on numerous occasions, one of which was on this day when passing Haydock Colliery Junction. Two NCB locos were shunting near the junction so I hung out of the window, aimed and fired. What absolute sheer good luck as nearest to the camera was none other than 0–6–0WT 'BELLEROPHON' built by the Haydock Foundry in 1874. It was the only representative of its type still working. Luckily it has been preserved and has been restored to operational condition. In the background just to the right of the Well tank behind the signal part of 0–6–0ST No.6 (P749/1898) can be seen. The signal is also a real gem. Maurice Dart/Transport Treasury.

We end with a couple of different industrial locos. At the Lancashire Electric Power Company's Kearsley Power station four overhead wire 4w + 4w electric locos were employed moving coal and ash around the site. Here is LEP 2 (HL 3872/1936) on site. From its clean appearance this was taken soon after the loco arrived. Steve Davies collection.

One of the stations near the top end of the branch line from Preston to Longridge was Grimsargh. From Grimsargh station a short branch line ran to Whittingham Mental Hospital. Two locos were used on the line. One was ex LBSCR 0–4–2T 2357 which became No.1 and was scrapped when worn out. The other was 4w VBTG No.2 'GRADWELL' (S 9377/1947) of 100hp which was purchased from Bolton Gas works. The line to the hospital closed on 30 June 1957 and on an unspecified date in 1958 'GRADWELL' and the rolling stock were in the Bay platform at Grimsargh station. The top edge of the nameplate can be seen just to the left of the raincoat hanging outside the cab.

LOCATION INDEX

Accrington 74, 105
Agecroft 117, 125
Aintree 18, 73
Alsager 44, 72
Altrincham 93
Astley Green Colliery 157
Bacup 128
Bank Hall 73, 101, 116-120
Bidston 16, 80
Birkenhead 68-70, 113
Blackpool 57, 61, 106, 107
Blackrod 103
Bolton 18, 23, 25, 38, 47, 49-51, 57, 58, 61, 72, 77, 78, 88, 96, 98, 100, 104, 125-127
Brackley Colliery 155, 156
Broadbottom viaduct 131
Burton & Holme 29
Burton Point 11, 15
Bury 127
Carnforth 43
Castleton 123
Chequerbent 20, 85
Chester 13, 35, 41, 46, 47, 51, 54, 63, 64, 66, 67, 82, 87, 94, 109, 112
Crewe 9, 13, 17, 27-37, 40-42, 46, 49, 50, 56, 60, 68, 69, 75, 76, 83, 89, 95, 110-112, 114, 121, 128, 133-135, 138-140, 142
Edge Hill 11, 29, 107, 115
Godley Junction 90
Gorton 10, 16, 26, 42, 79, 80, 91
Grimsargh 159
Guide Bridge 17, 45, 81
Haydock Colliery Junction 158
Hest Bank 33
Holcombe Brook 102
Horwich 75, 77, 78, 100, 102, 108, 117, 122, 124
Howe Bridge Colliery 158

Kearsley Power Station 159
Kirkham & Wesham 38, 44
Lees 24, 26, 58, 59
Liverpool Docks 115, 120, 144-153
Liverpool Overhead Railway 143, 144
Longsight 135
Lower Darwen 119
Lower Ince 62, 65
Lytham 128
Manchester 34, 43, 81, 82, 84, 86, 88-92, 94, 133, 136, 137, 139, 141, 142
Mersey Railway 129, 130
Mold Junction 12, 50
Morecambe 130
Mosley Common Colliery 156
Newton Heath 22, 23, 25, 55, 60, 74, 123
Northwich 14, 66, 93, 94
Parsonage Colliery 76
Patricroft 39, 83, 84
Peel Hall Opencast Site 157
Plodder Lane 47
Preston 28, 38, 39, 134
Preston Docks 118
Rose Grove 99
Southport 103
Speke Junction 15
Springs Branch 19, 21, 56, 59, 60, 63-65, 67
St Helens Junction 71
Sutton Oak 114
Torside 132
Trafford Park 54, 92, 104, 124
Walkden yard 52, 53, 153-155
Warrington 48, 55, 97, 101, 137, 141
Westhoughton 21, 87
Widnes 116
Wigan 22, 77, 136
Woodhead 132